TUTANKHAMUN

IN SEARCH OF
TUTANKHAMUN

Piero Ventura and Gian Paolo Ceserani

Silver Burdett Company
Morristown, New Jersey

In Search of Tutankhamun
Copyright © 1985 Arnoldo Mondadori Editore S.p.A.,
Milan
Translated from the Italian by Pamela Swinglehurst
Editor: Philip Steele
Design: Sally Boothroyd

First published in Great Britain in 1985 by
Macdonald & Co. (Publishers) Ltd.
London & Sydney

Adapted and published in the United States in 1985 by
Silver Burdett Company, Morristown, New Jersey.

Printed and bound in Spain by Artes Graficas Toledo S.A.
D. L. TO:1856-1987

Library of Congress Cataloging in Publication Data
Ventura, Piero.
  In search of Tutankhamun.

  Summary: Traces the search for and discovery of the
tomb of Tutankhamun and describes life in Egypt
during that pharaoh's rule.
  1. Tutankhamun, King of Egypt – Tomb – Juvenile
literature. 2. Excavations (Archaeology) – Egypt –
Valley of the Kings – Juvenile literature. 3. Valley
of the Kings (Egypt) – Antiquities – Juvenile literature.
4. Egypt – Antiquities – Juvenile literature.
[1. Tutankhamun, King of Egypt – Tomb. 2. Egypt –
Antiquities. 3. Egypt – Civilization – To 332 B.C.]

I. Ceserani, Gian Paolo, 1939-   II. Title.
DT87.5.V39 1985   932'.014   85-40416
ISBN 0-382-09122-1 (soft)
ISBN 0-382-09119-1 (lib. bdg.)

Contents

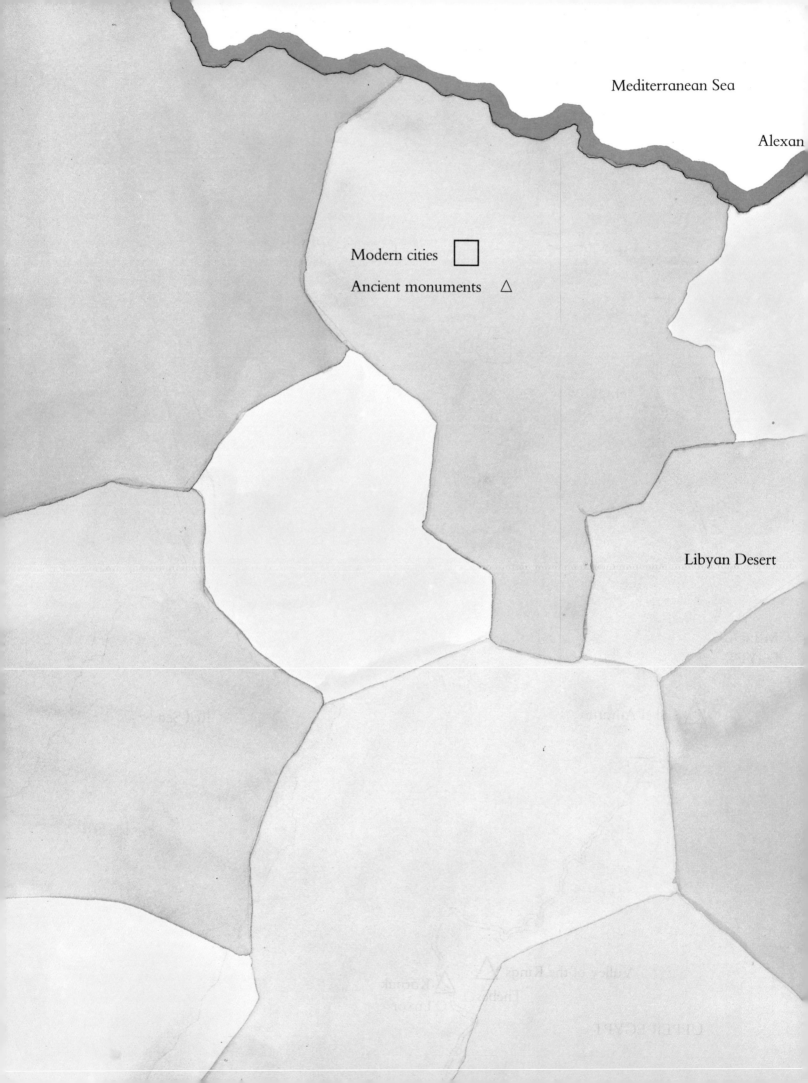

Mediterranean Sea

Alexan

Modern cities □
Ancient monuments △

Libyan Desert

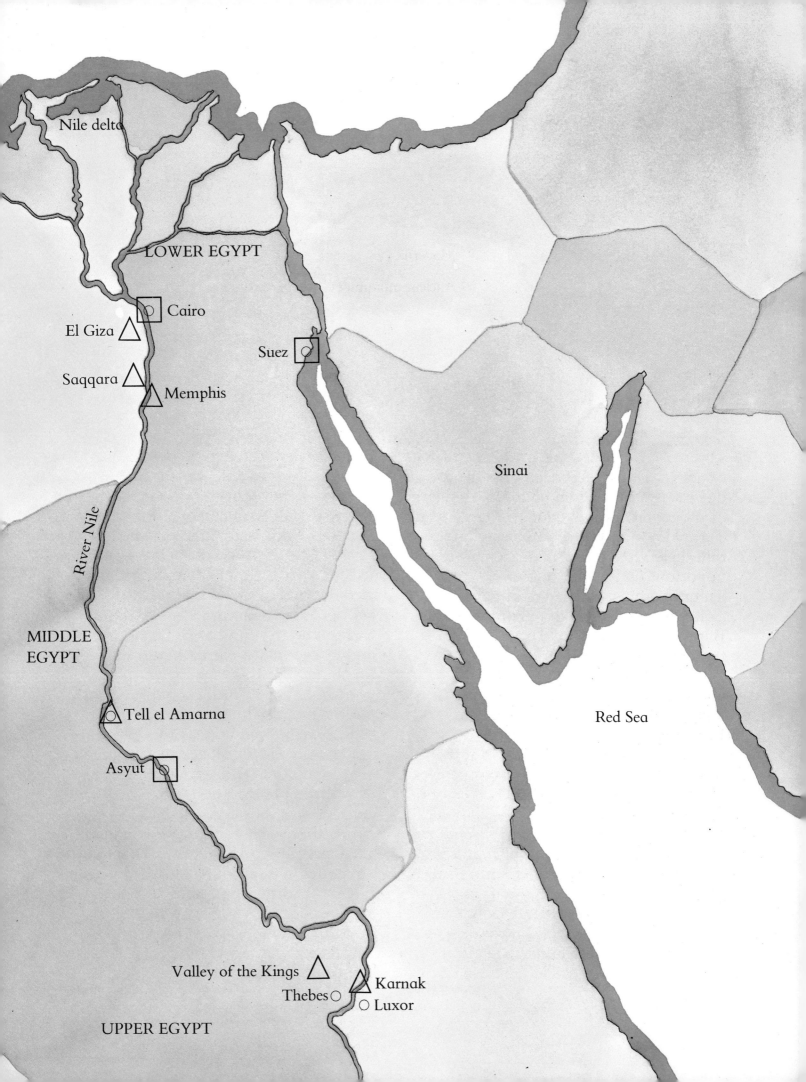

Nile delta

LOWER EGYPT

Cairo

El Giza

Suez

Saqqara

Memphis

Sinai

River Nile

MIDDLE
EGYPT

Tell el Amarna

Red Sea

Asyut

Valley of the Kings

Karnak

Thebes

Luxor

UPPER EGYPT

From Britain to Egypt

This story is about three men. The first two were British archaeologists. The third was an Egyptian pharaoh, and he died over 3000 years ago. His name was Tutankhamun. History books tell us that there were many pharaohs more important and powerful than Tutankhamun. He died at about eighteen, after a rule of only nine years. But today the name of Tutankhamun is famous all over the world.

In 1922 the burial place of this young pharaoh was discovered in a rocky valley near the River Nile. The two British archaeologists opened up the tomb, and there they found one of the most magnificent hoards of treasure ever seen in the world. Chambers carved out of solid rock were piled high with gold and jewelry, with statues and thrones. At the end of the search a splendid case was found, containing the mummified body of Tutankhamun himself.

As one precious object after another came to light, the archaeologists began to build up a picture in their minds of what life had been like in the distant past. An ancient secret had been revealed.

Before our story begins, we should take a look at the two men who had brought the world of ancient Egypt back to life in such a startling manner. One was a British lord – George Edward Stanhope Molyneux Herbert, the fifth Earl of Carnarvon. Lord Carnarvon was born in 1866. His family was very wealthy and he never had to work for a living. As a young man he preferred foxhunting to study. He loved to travel and visited South Africa, Australia, Japan and the United States.

In 1903 Lord Carnarvon visited Egypt for the first time. He had suffered a bad car accident, and was sent to Egypt for his health. There he became fascinated by the ruins of temples and tombs. He was given permission to excavate ancient sites, but he knew little about archaeology. He realized he would need an expert to work for him. Somebody suggested a man called Howard Carter.

Carter came from a very different background. He was born in the Norfolk village of Swaffham in 1873. His father was a draftsman. He could not afford to pay for his son's studies, so

he taught him to draw at home. Howard soon showed ability at copying detailed work, and he was sent to Egypt by the British Museum. At 17 years old he was already copying down the details of ancient temples and monuments. He learned a great deal about the history and art of ancient Egypt.

Howard Carter became a rather proud, conceited man. He often quarreled with his employers and lost his job. But Carter was stubborn too, and he was determined to stay in Egypt – the country where he had made his home. He became a tourist guide at one of the most important sites of ancient Egypt – the Valley of the Kings. It was not much of a job for someone of Carter's abilities. When the rich Lord Carnarvon offered him the job of director of excavations, he agreed right away.

In 1907 discoveries had been made in a place known as the Valley of the Kings. These offered a clue about where the tomb of the pharaoh Tutankhamun might be found. Howard Carter and Lord Carnarvon decided to start the search. World War One broke out in 1914, and it held up their plans for three years. At last in 1917 Carter could get down to work. For five long years he excavated rocks and sand and baked mud. He found nothing.

The Valley of the Kings

The Valley of the Kings is a desolate place. Few plants grow there. There are only cliffs and boulders, at the end of a rocky track. There is little shade to be found from the blazing sun. The valley lies to the west of the River Nile, about six miles from the ancient city of Thebes, near the modern town of Luxor.

Egypt used to be the richest and most powerful country in the world. For hundreds of years its rulers had been buried in magnificent tombs and huge pyramids. But then, over 3,500 years ago, the Egyptians began to bury their

pharaohs in this lonely spot at the edge of the desert. Why?

Ancient Egyptians believed in a life after death. In their tombs they piled up any objects that they thought the dead person might find useful in the other world. The royal tombs were strongrooms containing food and clothes, chariots and weapons, jewelry and gold. The tombs were sealed up, so nobody would ever see the treasure again.

But they did. Robbers broke into the tombs and ran off with the precious contents. One pharaoh, Tuthmosis I, decided that his tomb would be hidden in a secret spot robbers could not find. He chose the Valley of the Kings.

In search of Tutankhamun

Tuthmosis I carried out his plan. No robbers would take away all the treasure he needed after his death. Instead of a grand public monument he would have a hidden tomb which nobody knew about. It was dug in great secrecy, and when he died Tuthmosis was buried there with his treasure.

Other pharaohs followed his idea – including the boy-king Tutankhamun, who died sometime around 1344 BC. In all, 30 pharaohs came to be buried in the Valley of the Kings. Inside, the tombs were beautifully decorated and filled with the pharaoh's most magnificent possessions. Yet from the outside there was no way of telling that this was the site of great hoards of treasure.

The valley was guarded by royal servants – but it is hard to keep a secret for hundreds of years. Eventually, robbers did discover the tombs of the pharaohs. They would secretly slip into the valley by night, break the seals and plunder the tombs. Many poor peasants must have made their fortunes by selling the royal treasure.

Eventually the tombs stood empty. Thousands of years later, when archaeologists came to Egypt in search of the past, all that remained of the tombs were the walls, covered in beautiful paintings. Most people thought that the secrets of the valley had been lost centuries before. But not Howard Carter. He was sure that the valley held one last secret. All the clues pointed to one mysterious character: Tutankhamun. Nobody knew where he was buried.

Little was known about Tutankhamun. The pharaoh who reigned before him, however, was famous. This was Akhenaten, the first pharaoh in ancient Egypt who refused to worship all the ancient gods. He believed only one god, Aten, should be worshiped. He made enemies of the very powerful priests of Amun. Akhenaten built a new capital at Tell el Amarna and moved away from Thebes. He was married to a very beautiful queen called Nefertiti.

When Tutankhamun came to the throne, he took up the old religion once again. The capital was moved back to Thebes, and the priests of Amun became powerful once more. From his statues Tutankhamun seems to have been a handsome young man with fine features. His queen's name was Ankhesenamun. We know very few other details of his reign.

Howard Carter was sure that Tutankhamun lay buried somewhere in the Valley of the Kings. Yet why was there no mention of the tomb in any document? The ancient Egyptian judges had records made of the trials of grave robbers – but there was not a single mention of Tutankhamun's grave being plundered. Could it be possible that the grave robbers had never found it?

After five years of hard work, Howard Carter still had not found a tomb. Lord Carnarvon felt like giving up, but they decided to try one last time. On November 1, 1922, Carter started to dig once again, near the tomb of an important pharaoh called Rameses VI, which had been discovered a long time before.

The workers on the site were full of hope. Carter had brought a canary in a cage, and this became their mascot. They were sure they would be lucky this time. They were right. On the morning of November 4 the youngest worker on the site, a small boy, hit something hard in the sand. He dug furiously and uncovered a short flight of steps. The great discovery had begun!

Breaking the seals

There could be no possible doubt. The steps led deep down into the hillside. At last the workmen came to a walled-up doorway. Howard Carter's dream had come true.

There seemed to be no royal seal on the door, which was puzzling, but there were the seals of the valley guards. Carter covered up the doorway for safety, and sent a cable to Lord Carnarvon, who was in London at the time: "At last have made wonderful discovery in the Valley: a magnificent tomb with seals intact; recovered same for your arrival; congratulations."

Howard Carter waited for Lord Carnarvon to arrive. One day his

canary, the site's lucky mascot, was eaten by a cobra. The workmen thought their luck had run out, but Carter took no notice. Then on November 23 Lord Carnarvon arrived in Egypt with his daughter Evelyn.

Digging started again, and soon the whole entrance was uncovered and cleared of rubble. There at last were the missing royal seals – marked with the name of Tutankhamun. Carter noticed that the entrance showed definite signs of having been plundered, although the seals were unbroken. Perhaps the robbers had been caught red-handed by the valley guards thousands of years ago, and the tomb sealed up again.

The entrance was opened up and there was a passageway. It sloped downwards for 30 feet and was filled with rubble. As the workers cleared this away, they found some objects which had obviously come from the tomb. Perhaps the robbers had dropped them when they were discovered.

At the end of the passageway lay another blocked doorway. Here were more seals of Tutankhamun. The robbers had made an opening here as well, which had again been sealed by the guards. What could there be on the other side?

On November 26 four people stood in front of the second doorway. There was Lord Carnarvon and his daughter, an archaeologist called Callender and Howard Carter. For Carter, this was the most exciting day in his life. He made a small hole and held up a candle.

In the dark he could see the shapes of all kinds of objects, piled high. The room was glittering with gold.

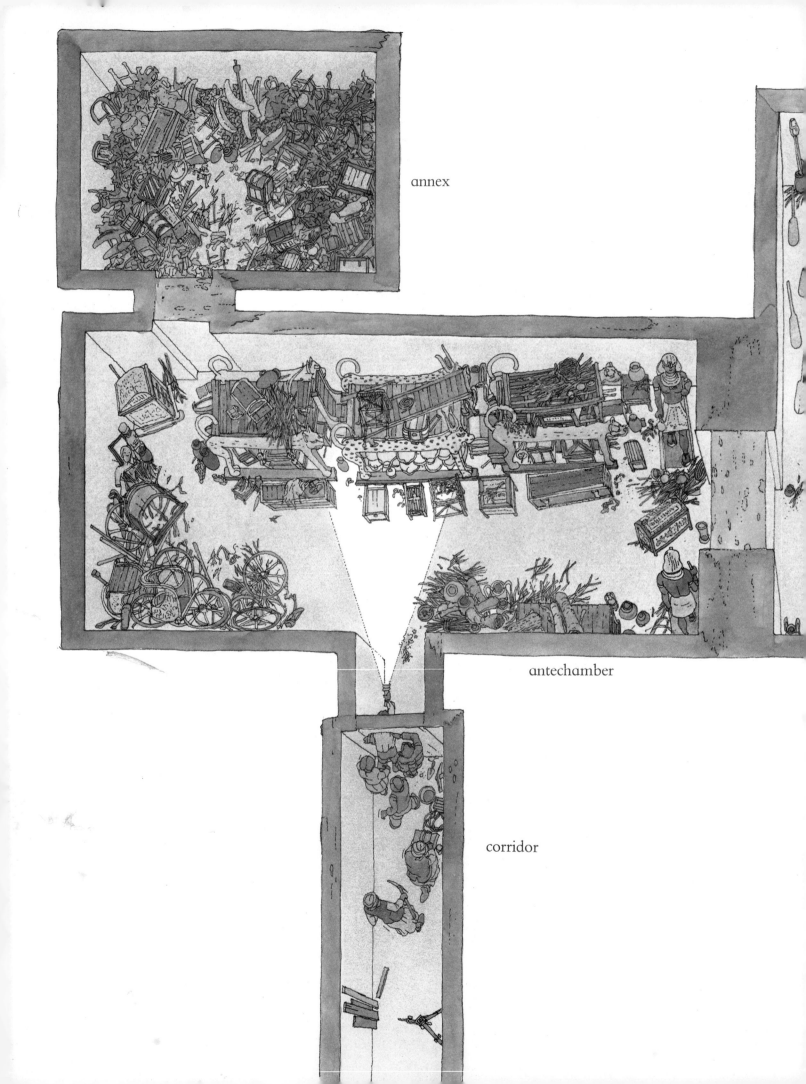

annex

antechamber

corridor

burial chamber

treasury

A journey in time

What was to be done? Howard Carter and his team were supposed to wait for the Egyptian officials to come before they entered the first room, called the "antechamber." In fact they climbed in secretly and had a look around. Could one really blame them?

They found they had traveled back in time over 3,000 years. There was the scent of oils, of perfumed ointments and wood. The room had a low ceiling about six feet long by eleven feet wide. Carter shone a torch over a dazzling array of treasure. Everything was in disorder – perhaps as a result of the robbers' visit 3,000 years before.

Along the walls were linen robes, chests and vases. There were four chariots which had been taken to pieces before being carried into the chambers. There were three beds in the form of animals, stools of ebony and gold and ivory. Carter and his group soon realized that blocked doors led off from the antechamber to other rooms.

The plan of the tomb was eventually to become clear. To the southeast was a small room which came to be called the "annex." To the north another doorway, guarded by statues of the king, led to the burial chamber itself. Here the space was filled by a huge wooden shrine covered in gold. To the east of this lay another room, which became known as the "treasury." Here was a statue of Anubis, the jackal-headed god, together with a golden shrine, chests and model boats.

It was to be many years before the whole tomb was emptied of its treasure, and all the objects carefully restored.

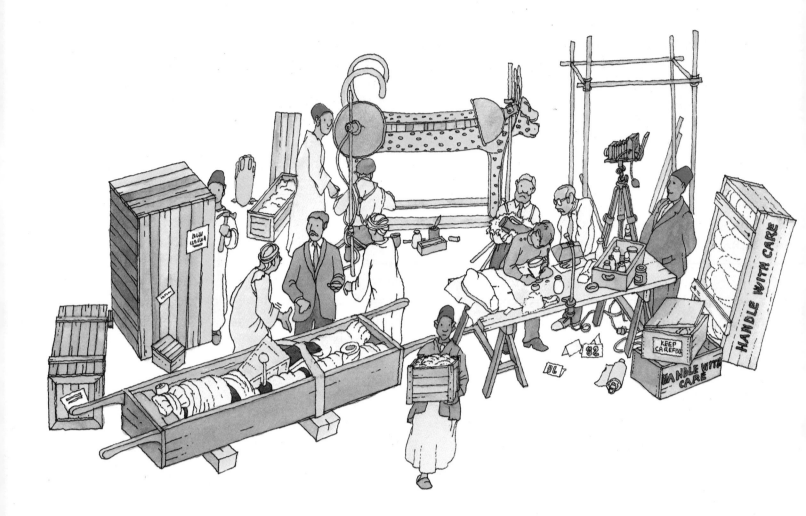

Recording and restoring

The news of Howard Carter's incredible discovery first appeared in London, in *The Times* newspaper. Soon the news was speeding around the world: the tomb of a mysterious Egyptian pharaoh had been discovered in the Valley of the Kings!

For Carter this was a difficult time. Letters and telegrams poured in from all over the world. Journalists and sightseers arrived every day from Luxor, traveling by car or on horseback. Ministers and officials, princes and important people all wanted to have a glimpse of the

tomb. Carter was a stubborn, serious man, and did not find it easy to deal with all these people. He risked making some powerful enemies.

Forty selected guests had been invited to the official opening of the tomb. Carter never told a soul that he had already explored the tomb on that first night. In front of his guests he solemnly reopened the blocked doorway. Everyone gazed wide-eyed at the treasures.

All Carter wanted to do was to get on with the really important job – the recording of all the objects in the tomb, and the restoration of the ancient treasures. He called in experts to help him. Photographers recorded everything as it was found, and every stage of the work in progress. Historians pored over the hieroglyphs, the picture writing of ancient Egypt. People from museums set about repairing and restoring furniture and cloth

The robbers who had broken into the tomb so many centuries before had caused a lot of damage. They had ripped out several of the gold decorations, and had used a crowbar to pry a layer of gold off the chariots. The main problem, however, was simply one of age. After more than 3,000 years everything was very brittle. When Carter picked up a pair of beautiful sandals they crumbled away, leaving only a few pieces of fabric and some pearls in his hand.

A laboratory was set up on the site, in the empty tomb of another pharaoh, Seti II. Here it was cool and sheltered. Carter found that the best way to preserve the treasures was to treat them with paraffin. The objects were photographed and treated, and then carried to the laboratory.

Crowds of curious visitors waited for hours, hoping for a glimpse of the treasure. The temperature would sometimes rise to 120 degrees F. From time to time a group of workmen would emerge from the darkness of the tomb, carrying a statue, a casket or a throne. The wealth of a forgotten age was seeing the light of day for the first time in thousands of years. The visitors peered, and their cameras clicked. The past was coming to life.

Kings, queens and curses

Visitors were arriving all the time. One day a procession of seven cars came up the valley, with a motorcycle outrider. Sixty years ago this was still a very unusual sight. Out stepped Elizabeth, Queen of the Belgians. She visited the tomb for an hour, and was so excited by what she saw that she stayed in Egypt for a month and paid three more visits to the tomb. A queen of the 20th century AD was paying homage to a king of the 14th century BC.

On February 26, 1923, work was stopped on the site for a time. A few weeks later, Lord Carnarvon was taken seriously ill. He had been bitten by a mosquito and the bite had become infected. He caught pneumonia and died on April 5, 1923.

Many people had been superstitious about the opening of Tutankhamun's tomb. The newspapers now began to say that Lord Carnarvon had died as the result of the pharaoh's curse. A lamp in the tomb had hieroglyphs on it saying: "It is I who protect the dead." All the lights in Cairo had gone out on the night he died. Some said he had been stabbed by a poisoned dagger, others that there had been deadly bacteria in the tomb. It was nonsense of course. Curses were anyway very rare in ancient Egypt. However the subject became a popular subject for horror stories and films for many years.

Things did not go well for Howard Carter. He quarreled with the Egyptian authorities about ownership of the treasures. He was depressed by the death of Lord Carnarvon, and never again felt as happy as he had at the moment of discovery.

In October, 1923, Carter returned to the site, ready to start work again. The burial chamber had been opened up in February: now it was time to open the shrine. Carter described this work as being like peeling the layers off an onion. There were four gold-covered shrines, one inside the other.

There was very little room to work in. The heat was stifling. When they reached the third shrine, everyone was dazzled by the brightness of the gold. At last they came to the final shrine. The excitement was unbelievable. Would they now find the sarcophagus, the case containing the coffin?

Howard Carter breathed a sigh of relief. Inside that final shrine lay the sarcophagus, a case of brown quartzite with a broken lid of granite. Carved upon it were the names and royal titles of Tutankhamun. This then was the final resting place of the king himself. Inside the sarcophagus was the mummified body of the pharaoh.

The king is found

Archaeologists have to be very patient people. Nothing is done in a hurry. They must be careful and make sure no mistakes are made. By February 12, 1924, Howard Carter was ready to lift the heavy stone lid off the sarcophagus.

Twenty-four people crowded into the tomb to watch. The sarcophagus was opened and the lights revealed a splendid coffin. It was made of wood covered in shining gold and carved in the shape of the young pharaoh. It was studded with colored glass and pottery.

Where was the mummy? They had to wait a long time to find out. Carter argued with the Egyptian government, and then he went abroad – to the United States. There he told everyone about his discoveries. Tutankhamun had become very famous. After a year, Howard Carter decided to go back to Egypt. He made his peace with the government, and started work again.

But the mysterious mummy was not found right away. Inside the coffin was another gold-covered coffin in the shape of the pharaoh. This too was opened.

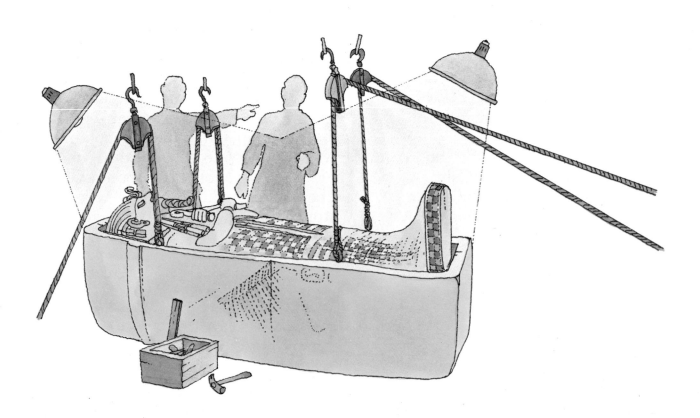

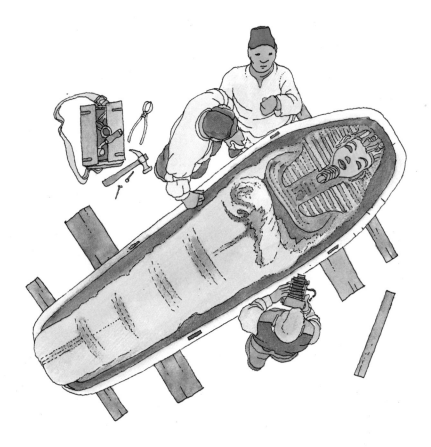

Inside that was a *third* coffin. This was made of solid gold, about one inch thick. It was beautifully decorated.

Carter opened this third coffin, and removed the cloth covering, the shroud. Looking back at him was a shimmering gold mask decorated with glass and precious stones. The face was young and handsome, and very peaceful. Beneath the mask were the bandages of the mummy, the dried, embalmed body of Tutankhamun.

Carter began to cut away the bandages, but they crumbled to dust. Among the bandages were no less than 143 of the king's personal treasures: necklaces, bracelets and jewels.

The body itself was not in a good condition, but scientists were able to treat it. It seemed that the pharaoh must have been about 18 when he died, and that he had probably been about five and a half feet tall. How had Tutankhamun died? Had be been ill, or had he been murdered? We do not know, and we may never learn the truth.

The king had been found, but the scientists were able to tell us little more than the historians. Tutankhamun may not have been an important pharaoh in his day, but his fame lived on for 32 centuries. This little-known pharaoh became the wonder of the world.

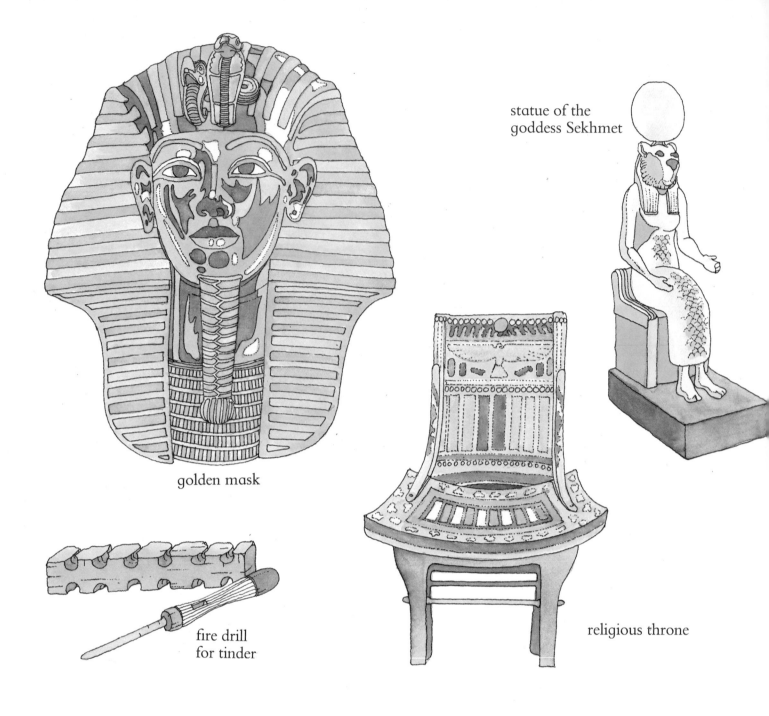

golden mask

statue of the
goddess Sekhmet

fire drill
for tinder

religious throne

A pharaoh's treasure

Carter's work was not over yet. He still
had to examine all the objects in the
rooms known as the annex and the
treasury: chairs, caskets, shrines and
sacred objects. The work continued until
1932. Each treasure was carefully
packed up in containers and pushed
along rails to the banks of the River
Nile.

From here they were taken by boat or
train to Cairo, the modern capital of
Egypt. They found a new home in the
museum there, where they may still be
seen today. Tutankhamun's body was
reburied in the tomb.

Howard Carter went back to Britain.
He was to return to Egypt, but not to
the Valley of the Kings. The man who
had found the most incredible treasure

Shu head rest

earring

gaming board

camp bed

the pharaoh
on a leopard

hoard the world had ever seen died on
March 2, 1939.

From the Cairo Museum
Tutankhamun's treasures were sent
around the world. In Chicago alone a
million people came to look at them.
They were sent to England, to France, to
the Soviet Union. Everywhere people
lined up for hours and hours to see them.
They gazed at the golden mask, the
thrones, stools and beds, the chariots,
the statues, the jewels.

In more recent years another world
tour showed off Tutankhamun's treasure
to millions more. The riddle of the
pharaoh might have been solved by
Howard Carter, but to many people the
discovery had simply posed further
questions. Who were the ancient
Egyptians? How had they lived? What
kind of people had produced such
wonders? More and more people became
interested in this ancient civilization.

The land of the dead

Why did the ancient Egyptians place so much importance on death? Why did they fill their tombs with treasure and bury such beautiful things underground? Over the ages, Egypt seems to have given its wealth to the dead rather than the living. Why?

A funeral procession like the one in the picture was not in fact a sad occasion, for everyone believed a new life had begun when the person had died. Belief in life after death was so strong, that it seemed only natural to take one's possessions along on the final journey of all. Ancient Egyptians enjoyed life just as we do, but believed that if the funeral was arranged correctly, the dead person could live on in a sunny, happy land.

The Egyptians believed that every person had several souls. One of them was a personal spirit – the *ka*. When someone died, most of these souls left the body. In the afterlife they took on various forms, such as that of a bird with a human head. The *ka*, however, stayed attached to the body, which it looked after.

A dead body had to be preserved properly, or the *ka* would be destroyed along with the body. This was why the ancient Egyptians mummified dead bodies. Corpses were prepared with special ointments and bandages. Embalmed in this way, the mummies of humans – and animals too – have survived for thousands of years.

Tutankhamun's tomb was filled with furniture, means of transportation such as chariots and boats, with clothes, food and cups. There were weapons, and gaming boards to while away the time. His body was mummified. In this way the boy king was prepared for life in the next world, his *ka* by his side for ever.

27

The river people

If you look at a map of Africa, you will see that Egypt is a land of deserts. Most of the country is made up of sand and rock. It is a very hot land in which little grows. Through this dry landscape runs the longest river in the world – the Nile.

Far to the south, there are two Niles. One river, the Blue Nile, carries water from the mountains of Ethiopia. The other, the White Nile, has its source in the great lakes of central Africa. The two rivers join near the modern city of Khartoum, in Sudan.

From there they form a single waterway which flows north through the deserts of Egypt. At the end of its journey the Nile splits into a number of smaller streams, forming a delta at the coast of the Mediterranean Sea. In Tutankhamun's day, the people of Egypt depended on the river for survival.

Every year in June the River Nile would flood and cover the land on either side. The waters would then go down very slowly until, by November, the river was back to its normal size. As the waters receded they left behind a layer of mud. Over the ages this became a rich soil, renewed every year.

About 6,000 years ago people began to farm this strip of land along the Nile valley. Channels were dug to carry river water into the countryside for the irrigation of crops. The river brought wealth and power.

Cities grew up such as Memphis and Thebes. Huge monuments were built, pillars, statues and pyramids. Pharaohs ruled over splendid courts, and priests worshiped in magnificent temples. For over 2,500 years Egypt was the center of the known world. This was the home of Tutankhamun: the land of the great river.

29

Everyday living

In ancient Egypt everyday life was controlled by the flow of the river. When would the flood arrive? How big would it be? As soon as the waters receded the farmers would start to work the land.

Oxen were used to pull wooden plows, and seed was sown. At the end of March the corn was ready to be harvested. The river was a source of food in itself. Large nets were used to catch fish from the Nile. Waterfowl were also netted at the river's edge. Most families would keep a few ducks, geese, chickens or rabbits. Roasted in the open air, they would provide an occasional feast.

The ancient Egyptians did not have a very varied diet. There were always bread, onions and fish on the table. And

they also ate lentils, peas and chick peas. Fruit included grapes, figs, dates and pomegranates. Goats and cows provided milk and cheese. The Egyptians loved eating ring-shaped cakes and biscuits which they sweetened with honey.

Sugar was unknown, of course, as was other foreign produce such as maize, beans, potatoes, peaches, melons, cherries, oranges and lemons.

Life was very hard for the peasant working in the field. The building of irrigation channels meant that people had to work together from the earliest times. Rulers and priests were able to organize a large work force for their building works. These could be carried out during the season of the flood, when the farmland was under water.

Thousands of people would toil away under the hot sun. They would carry huge slabs of stone and make bricks from mud. They were not always cruelly treated. It seems they received a fair wage, and had certain rights – for instance, they were allowed to go on strike. Sometimes competitions were organized, and prizes given to the best workers.

When the building was finished the workers would return to their riverside homes. For poor peasants, these were simple huts made of reeds or mud bricks. They provided little more than shelter. In a hot climate, however, people spend a lot of time outdoors. The peasants worked and sat in their yards, or on the flat roofs of buildings.

Life was more comfortable for the nobles and the officials of the royal court. They lived in houses with halls, reception rooms, guest rooms and even bathrooms. Some had gardens, swimming pools and stables. Their servants cooked their food for them and carried their water.

For the peasants it made little difference who was pharaoh and who was not. For thousands of years the waters would rise and fall, the seed would be sown and the crops harvested. Even today, along the banks of the Nile, the ancient way of life has changed very little.

The god-king

The pharaoh lived in a fine palace, with everything he could possibly want. From here he governed the empire. He had all kinds of duties and religious ceremonies to carry out.

From an early age the future pharaoh would be prepared for the throne. He would have the best possible teachers, and learn about religion and how to rule. Sometimes the priests and court officials remained very powerful throughout the pharaoh's reign. This would seem to have been the case at the time of Tutankhamun.

The pharaoh was expected to show how brave he was during wars, and to be a skillful hunter. A fan found in Tutankhamun's tomb has a picture of an ostrich hunt in which the young king took part. Sometimes pharaohs hunted elephants and lions. Today these

animals are only found far to the south of Egypt, in the Sudan.

The pharaoh ruled everybody and everything in Egypt. Why was he given such power? According to the religion of the ancient Egyptians, the pharaoh was a living god – the living form of Horus, the offspring of Osiris. He was god of the living and the dead, and was the high priest as well. It is easy to see why the funeral of Tutankhamun was such a splendid affair.

The pharaoh was also head of state and commander of the army. All the glory came to him. On buildings, memorials, records of victories, there is always only one name – that of the pharaoh. Sometimes a pharaoh would try to remove all references to another pharaoh, and so take away their immortality. After Tutankhamun died the pharaoh Horemheb tried to do just this – but luckily he did not destroy the tomb.

god	baby	woman	man	wild beast	worm	fish	bird
goose	cow	sacred bark	boat	tree	flower	water	sail
wood	corn	seed	desert	road	embrace	force	mouth
plow	sarcophagus	eye	star	sun	metal	stone	sand
go	go back	cobra	scarab	fly	lizard	turtle	crocodile
frog	falcon	vulture	bow	prince	priest	enemy	defeated enemy
conceive	feed	nobleman	servant	messenger	give birth	wet nurse	mummy
king	guardian	foreigner	eat	worship	hide	tired	work
brewer	friend	soldier	house	shrine	head	feast	fire
earth	city	tie	sky	hair	night	street	drink

cartouches of the pharaohs

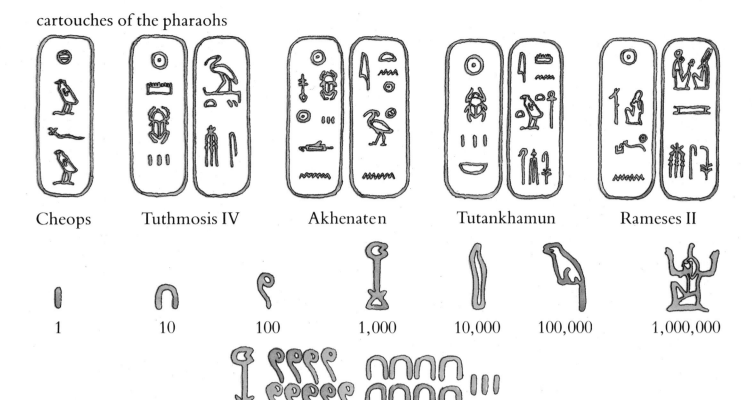

| Cheops | Tuthmosis IV | Akhenaten | Tutankhamun | Rameses II |

1   10   100   1,000   10,000   100,000   1,000,000

1983

Writing in pictures

Howard Carter and other archaeologists working in Egypt had to study hieroglyphs, the picture writing of the ancient Egyptians. Various forms of writing had been used in Egypt, and until the last century nobody was able to understand them.

There were over 3,000 hieroglyphic symbols. Some of them, such as "cobra" or "star" were easy to recognize. But others seemed to represent sounds, as do the letters of our alphabet today.

The code was broken by a lucky accident. In 1798 the French general, Napoleon Bonaparte, invaded Egypt. Along with his troops came French scholars, who were the first people in modern times to make accurate drawings of the ancient monuments.

One day a French officer found a slab of black stone near Rosetta, on the Nile delta. Some words were written on it in hieroglyphics – and underneath this, the same words appeared in the alphabet of ancient Greece. People could understand Greek, the letters could be compared.

Even so, it was no easy task. It took 23 years to crack the code, and it was a genius who finally did it. Jean François Champollion was a French scholar. When he was only 11 he had been able to understand most of the languages of Europe. At the age of 19 he was a professor of history at the University of Grenoble. He was determined to find out the secret of the Rosetta Stone.

Night after night Champollion tried to solve the problem. At last he was successful. Scholars could work out a system of hieroglyphics. They decided when a symbol referred to a particular object, and when it meant a sound. Howard Carter and his team could follow the clues which led them to Tutankhamun.

The master builders

If you travel through Egypt today you will see many huge buildings which are still standing after thousands of years. There are the mighty pyramids at El Gizeh outside Cairo. The highest is that of Cheops. It is 475 feet high, and each side measures over 750 feet at the base.

There are fantastic temples such as that at Karnak, near Thebes. There are tall obelisks ("needles" of stone) and colossal stone figures such as those of Memnon at Thebes.

Some years ago a new dam was built on the River Nile, at Aswan in southern Egypt. The temples at Abu Simbel had to be taken down and rebuilt if they were to be saved from the rising water level. It took all the skill of modern engineers to carry out the task. Despite all their machines and their knowledge of modern technology, they found it a very difficult job indeed. So how did the ancient Egyptians manage?

They had no metal tools. They had to use stone chisels and wooden mallets. They had no cranes or winches. They did know about the wheel – but they did not use it for transport. The great blocks of stone were carried by boat, and then hauled on sledges by men with ropes. We still do not really understand how

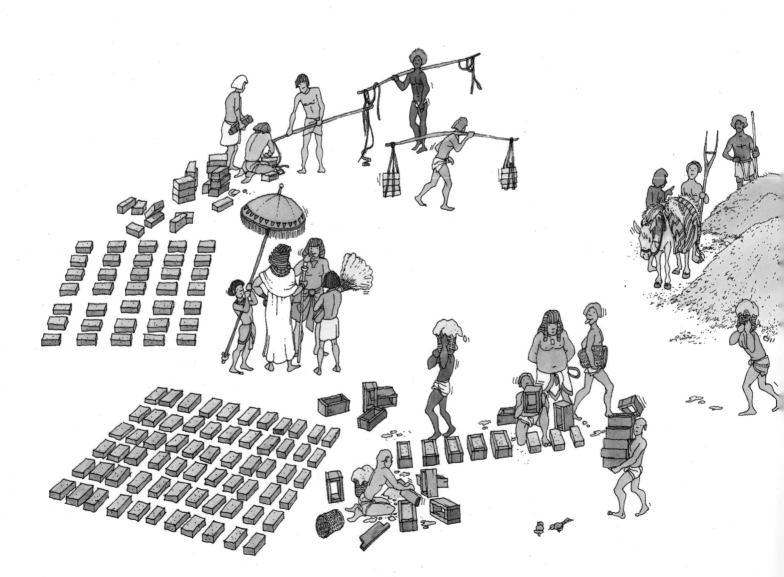

a monument such as the pyramid of Cheops was built. We do know that it was made up of over two million slabs, each one weighing over two tons. Slabs were split by driving in wooden wedges. These were soaked in water until they swelled up and cracked the stone. Just how the slabs were raised to a height of more than 300 feet is a mystery.

The building of this pyramid must have taken about 20 years. Maybe as many as 100,000 people toiled away to build this king's tomb, swarming like ants across the empty desert. The ancient Egyptians were some of the best engineers the world has ever seen. By the time of Tutankhamun, of course, the royal tombs were hidden away. But the great building works still went on.

Only special buildings were made of stone. Houses, walls and fortresses were made of mud bricks. A mixture of soil and water was trampled and churned into mud in a big pit. Straw and sand were added for strength. The mixture was then pressed into wooden molds and left to dry in the sun for a week. Bricks are still made in this way in many parts of the world today. They are good and strong, but they do not last for thousands of years, like the stone slabs of the pyramids.

The pyramid is meant to be a memorial to the great pharaoh. It is also a memorial to the thousands of ordinary people who lived and died building it.

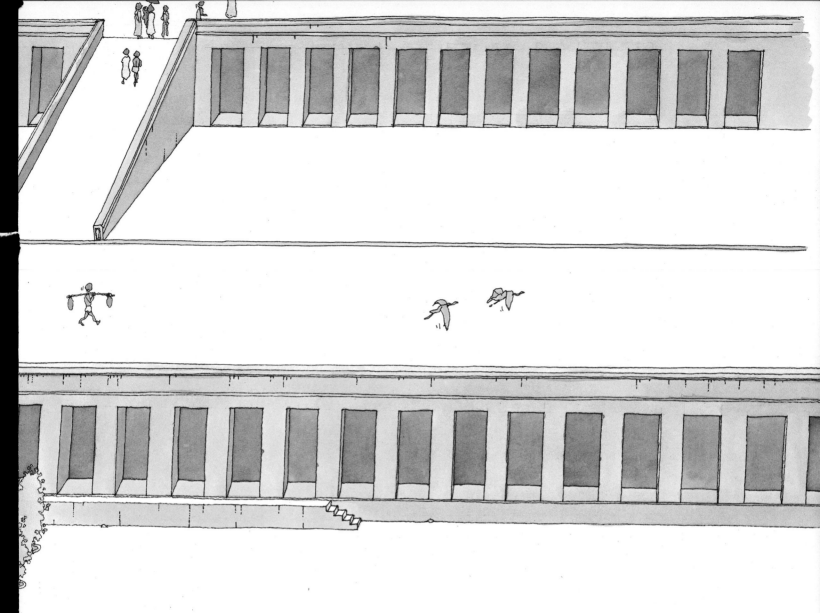

Temples and shrines

The center of religious life in ancient Egypt were the temples. Many of these magnificent buildings still stand today. While the pyramids were built in a relatively short time, the temples grew up over hundreds of years, and were added to and altered.

Some temples were built to honor the dead, but most of them were built for the gods. They were not places of worship, like churches or mosques are today. They were places where the god actually lived. In each temple there was a shrine containing the god's statue.

Where was the god to be found? Not in the entrance halls, courtyards, store rooms and towers around the outside. To reach the shrine of the god you had to make your way through a series of doors to the very center of the building. Each room was smaller and darker than the one before. The last room was tiny and airless. It had no windows. Here was the life-giving statue of the god.

The statue of the god was rarely removed from the shrine. But sometimes a procession would be held, and the idol would be carried through the streets in a boat made of gold.

Gods and goddesses

Every day the priests of the temple would wash, dress and even make up the statues of the gods. People would give the priests food such as bread, cakes and meat. They would eat this on behalf of the god.

The ancient Egyptians probably had over 3,000 gods and goddesses. Each village had its own, but some were more important than others. Many of them were linked with particular animals. Khnum, for instance, was shown with the head of a ram. Thoth had the head of an ibis, and Anubis that of a jackal. Animals sacred to the gods were mummified when they died, just like humans.

As in ancient Greece and Rome, there were gods and goddesses which represented the sun (Ra), the sky (Nut), the air (Shu), and the earth (Geb). Maat was the goddess of truth and justice. During Tutankhamun's reign the most important god was Amun, after whom the pharaoh was named.

The Egyptians enjoyed telling stories about their gods. One of these was about Osiris, the god of the dead, who also taught people how to farm, how to forge metals and how to build. His wife was Isis, the great goddess who could cure illness and teach people how to bake, weave and sew.

Osiris had a wicked brother, Seth, who was jealous of him. During a feast Seth showed his guests a jewel-studded casket. He promised to give it to anyone who could fit inside it. Osiris was not suspicious: he squeezed in. Right away

Shu, the god of the air, holds up the sky goddess, Nut. At his feet lies Geb, the earth god.

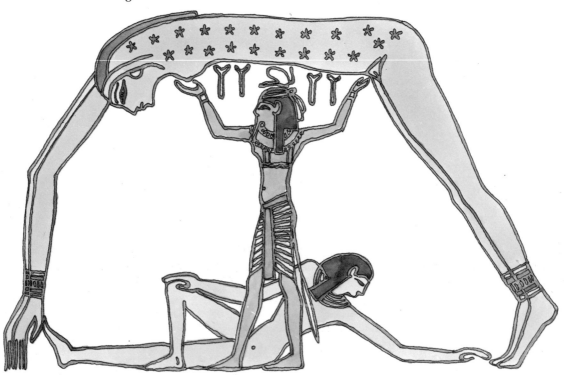

Maat

Khnum   Amun   Thoth   Isis   Anubis

Seth sealed him inside the casket and threw it in the Nile.

The casket became trapped by magic in a tree. The tree was made into a column at the king's palace in Byblos. Isis came to Byblos in search of Osiris. Every night she would fly around the column letting out heart-rending cries. At last she managed to find her husband's body.

The evil Seth stole it back from her. He cut it into 14 pieces which he hid all over Egypt. Again Isis came to the rescue, and brought Osiris back to life.

Priests and learning

The priests were some of the most important and powerful people in Egypt. They organized the worship of the gods, and served in the temples. They had three religious services a day, one in the morning, one at noon, and one in the evening. They looked after the statues of the gods and said prayers.

A Greek historian called Herodotus visited Egypt in the 5th century BC. He wrote that the Egyptian priests had to wash in cold water four times a day. Shaving the head was common practice in ancient Egypt: the priests had to do this every two days – and pluck their eyebrows and eyelashes as well!

The priests often played an important part in the life of the court, as at the time of Tutankhamun. They also did a lot more besides. For example they were very skillful doctors. Herodotus was amazed by their knowledge. They even had doctors who specialized in certain medical problems as doctors do today.

The Egyptian priest-doctors were famous throughout the ancient world. They carried out operations, set broken bones, stitched wounds, and used medicines and a sort of sticky plaster. Archaeologists have been amazed by the fine teeth of many mummies. Decayed teeth were filled, and loose teeth bound with gold thread.

When it came to science, the priests were without equal. About 2800 BC King Zoser had a doctor called Imhotep. This priest was also a brilliant architect, and he is said to have built the great step-pyramids at Saqqara. He was so famous that over 2,000 years later the Egyptians were worshiping him as a god!

In ancient Egypt a knowledge of

astronomy was very important. By gazing at the sky the priests were able to record the movement of the sun and moon, and the position of stars and planets. They worked out a calendar of 365 days per year and 24 hours per day. By 1528 BC this calendar was perfect. When should farmers sow their seed? When was the Nile expected to flood? The priests knew all the answers.

Egypt at war

The Egyptian empire never covered a very large area, like the Roman empire. It was largely a land of deserts. There were, however, many wars. Some were fought between people from different parts of Egypt, some were fought against foreign invaders. The borders were always guarded.

We know from pictures that the armies were well trained. Weapons included spears and shields, bows and arrows. Ladders and battering rams were used to conquer enemy fortresses. Even so, Egypt was sometimes defeated. Around 1720 BC it was invaded by the Hyksos people. They were experts at using chariots in battle.

When the Egyptians threw off Hyksos rule, they kept the chariot as a battle weapon. Chariots were pulled by two horses and a driver and an archer rode behind. The chariot had to be light in order to run at speed over sand. Thanks to the Tutankhamun discovery, we now know exactly what they were like.

The land of riddles

It sometimes seems that the more we find out about ancient Egypt, the less we know. Visitors to Egypt are overawed by what they see. There is one great sphinx at El Giza. It has the body of a lion, and the head of a pharaoh, wearing the headdress known as a *nemset*. For thousands of years it has stared out across the sand of the desert.

Behind the sphinx is the great pyramid of Cheops. Inside it a huge, empty sarcophagus was found, made of granite. Such monuments seem just as magical and mysterious to us today as they must have seemed to the people of ancient Egypt so many years ago.

The discovery of Tutankhamun's tomb has helped us to find out all kinds of things about the way of life in ancient Egypt. Some of the mysteries have been solved. But what of the pharaoh himself? We still know very little.

By a strange coincidence we do know what happened immediately after his death. In the records of the Hittite people there is a reference to a letter received by their King Suppiluliuma in 1349 BC. It was from Ankhesenamun – Tutankhamun's widow. She was begging for the hand of one of his sons in marriage. She had no children and was now afraid of being married to a court official. Sadly the marriage never took place. For a time she reigned together with the elderly Ay, who may have been her grandfather. He was succeeded by the pharaoh Horemheb.

It was Horemheb who tried to destroy all trace of Tutankhamun. And it was thousands of years later that Howard Carter and Lord Carnarvon made sure that the name of Tutankhamun would become one of the most famous in history. The rest of the story is lost in time.